Social Media Marketing

Proven Strategies To Make Big Money Online

Jerry Shoemaker

SOCIAL MEDIA MARKETING

To define the term Social Media Marketing let's first analyze the definition of each word that makes up the term itself. The word 'social' implies that communication is happening between two parties and the term 'media' is simply the platform or method by which people are 'doing' social. And 'marketing' is the act of promoting products and services that lead to sales opportunities.

To summarize, Social Media Marketing is the process of promoting people, brands, products or services using Social Media platforms such as Facebook, Twitter, YouTube, LinkedIn, etc. While the principles of marketing remain, the strategies and psychology of marketing on each platform can be vastly different.

From a business perspective, each Social Media website serves one or more purposes as a marketing medium, the use of which depends on the target market you wish to communicate with (and sell to).

Social media marketing is the savvy marketers' use of social media to build a relationship with their existing and potential customers. In today's 'flat' world, cheap and easy-to-use tools like Facebook and LinkedIn have been bringing together a large community of people for a few years now. It is only recently that businesses have realized the potential of such communities as places to make themselves known in a crowded marketplace where a huge number of vendors are jostling for space.

The use of social media is not a new phenomenon. People have been using technology for gathering information and for socializing for over thirty years. The telephone 'phreaking' of the sixties and seventies, the BBS (bulletin board system) of the nineties and then the World Wide Web became popular means to meet and connect with people. But it wasn't until a few years ago that the flurry of tools like Twitter, Facebook and YouTube started being used to promote brands and products.

The Nielsen Report has found the popularity of social media in the global scenario has been growing day by day. Along with this report, other studies have found that more and more people are being influenced. Businesses are learning how to take advantage of this. They create their respective brands. The brands are personalized on these platforms. Consumers 'follow' the brands and are introduced to new products when these are launched. In this way the brands can become a part of their customers' everyday lives.

Marketing on the social media platform has to be a regular activity however. If we, as business owners, are not regular in our interactions with our 'friends' and 'followers', then they will soon lose interest. There are a number of firms that offer marketing services to help companies build their social media image. Large companies usually have the funds to hire them that small companies may not. However that doesn't mean that these small companies cannot benefit from marketing.

The ⬜uestion people look for on the web is "what is social media marketing?" Many people should first know what these web-pages are? Social media, in simpler terms, is communicating or sharing to people or the public through the web or on a mobile device. People share gossip, ideas, news, or anything they wish to share to one another. The most popular forms of social sites are blogs, forums, and social network sites, like Facebook.

How does marketing fit in with social media? People who are users of Facebook and twitter always talk to one another through messaging. They talk about anything from who's wearing what to interior decorating and so on. Marketers can put their ad on these sites and before you know it your product or service will go viral in minutes. Twitter allows people to post a micro-blog entry or a tweet. A person might tweet about a new pair of shoes they bought by posting the link of the product in their entry. Facebook works pretty much the same way except through more than just a link, but videos, advertisements, and photos.

What is social media marketing to large businesses? Large companies like Microsoft, Wal-Mart, Best Buy, and other businesses use these sites for marketing purposes. If businesses have their own Facebook page they can easily promote their products and services. When a person sees that company's page they will become fans of that page and refer other people to see them on Facebook. Marketing for twitter is pretty much the same as Facebook. Companies that who use twitter will put an entry, or tweet on their account for any new products or services that they just released.

Social network marketing has also become very efficient and mobile. What is social media marketing to mobile devices? Mobile phones and computer tablets, also known as touch pads, are been used many times for these websites. When you are away from your computer or laptop they are proven very efficient. This makes marketing easier than ever. Imagine a person who is going shopping and has their phone on them. If they are looking for some sales going on at target they can just simply go their Facebook or twitter page and look there.

Social media marketing has taken internet marketing to a whole new level. Before, ads got displayed on major search engines like Google, yahoo and others. Today, social sites are the new marketing platform for marketers. What is social media marketing? It is the next best thing in online marketing.

What is it exactly?

Social networking is all around us. From YouTube to Facebook, it is easier than ever to spread your marketing message to everyone and anyone who will listen. It succeeds by utilizing word of mouth marketing and focusing on building relationships, engaging consumers and interacting with them. This builds trust and furthers communication, increasing the circulation of your marketing message.

Social Media Marketing & Social Presence

One of the first steps in achieving success is having a solid foundation on which to begin with. This will be your social media presence. By developing a presence, you are essentially creating a following of people who will be interested in your brand's message later on. By doing this your message can be strictly content based, because your brand's social media presence has already drawn in your target market.

What are the benefits?

Social media has many benefits but the major selling point for any company is how such a low cost operation can reach millions of targeted consumers worldwide. This high ROI is what initially lures companies towards it. Once they are on board, a slew of other benefits become apparent. Some of those benefits include more developed relationships with consumers, easy implementation into current marketing strategies, free word of mouth advertising and becoming part of a vast online community, among other benefits. The longer you leave content in social media space, the higher your ROI will be! For example, by leaving you content available on a blog or social networking site, you would have no extra costs and consumers would be still able to continuously view your message.

Different Types

When most people think social media, a few big names come to mind, such as Facebook, Twitter and LinkedIn, but more and more options of marketing outlets are becoming available. These different outlets allow companies to specifically target groups of consumers who frequent those sites. A great example of this would be distributing a cat food marketing message through the use of multiple pet forums. Using this method can help pinpoint exactly where to spread your text or video content. It also allows you to reach target consumers without wasting time on people without pets. Through content creation, online video, viral marketing and social apps it is becoming much easier to spread a message through social media.

Examples of Social media platforms:

Facebook

Facebook, the most popular of the Social Media websites has essentially two sides. Firstly, from a purely social perspective, it allow any individual to join and find, connect and communicate with anybody they choose, whether they be existing friends, school or university colleagues, family members, work colleagues and more.

The second side to Facebook is the business side. Facebook allows the creation of a 'Facebook Page' to anyone, but for business owners, they represent an opportunity to promote their products and services.

A Facebook Page is now an essential marketing tool for businesses of all shapes and sizes. They allow businesses the ability to attract 'fans' (past, present or future customers) as well as interact with these fans on the Facebook Page itself, primarily on the 'Wall' page.

A Facebook Page has multiple pages just like a normal business website would. The default pages contained within a brand new Facebook Page are; Wall, Info, Photos.

Business owners can also setup advertising within Facebook to drive visitors to the business's Facebook Page as a way of attracting more customers.

Twitter

Twitter is what's known as a 'Micro-Blog'. Micro meaning small and a Blog is like a news-feed containing information about a person, company, topic, industry etc., etc.

Twitter allows you to 'post' information of 140 characters in length about anything you wish. While it's true purpose is unknown it serves as a broadcast medium for businesses, individuals, celebrities or anyone who wants to voice their option or expertise about any subject they choose.

YouTube

YouTube is a video sharing website and due to its popularity and vast resource of information on just about any topic you can imagine, has become the second largest search engine (after Google). This means that people use YouTube to search for video content about any topic they wish to search for. It's no doubt that online video one of the primary ways our society uses as a way to communicate, learn, share and engage with others.

YouTube allows anyone the ability to upload a video of their choosing onto their own YouTube account for public or private viewing.

LinkedIn

LinkedIn serves two purposes. The first, it's a way for job seekers (or employers) to connect with each other.

Secondly, it's a business tool that allows business owners the ability to connect with and build a 'network' of contacts. Thinking of it like a business networking group, located online.

You can use LinkedIn to be introduced to someone via an existing contact in your network. It can be a powerful tool if your business is B2B.

Your choice of Social Media platform to choose to market yourself, your company or your products and services should be dictated by the type of customer you wish to connect with as well as the type of engagement and interaction you wish to have with the person.

More details about Social Media Marketing

As far as price is concerned, there is no other low-cost method out there that will deliver a large number of visitors, whom can come back to your website again and again.

Whether you are selling products or services, or just publishing content for ad revenue, the efficiency and benefits of social media marketing is an unmatched method that will make your website profitable over time.

Social News Websites:

The benefits of a social media website vary, but a proven method is creating viral content and promoting it through social media channels. Link Baits, otherwise known as content created for the purpose of getting people to link to it, are a great start. Successful link baits are not hard to accomplish - you just have to know how to do it. Creating high quality content and then getting it listed on social media websites like Digg and StumbleUpon will lead to a number of benefits for any website.

There are two methods to this madness:

• Primary and Secondary Traffic: Primary traffic is the number of visitors who come directly from social media websites. Secondary traffic is the referral traffic that comes from websites that link to your content and ultimately sends you visitors back to your website.

• High Quality Links: Social News websites, like Digg or Reddit will get you a large number of links - that have the possibility, with high quality editorial content, to bring you traffic and ultimately raise your ranking in search engines.

There is no secret to this. As SEO has taking a bashing over the past few years - many SEO firms and specialist battle back and forth on the importance of keywords, Meta tags, link purchasing -you name it, they have fought over it. In the end though, the secret isn't that hard to uncover, quality content, sewn together with valuable keywords and building inbound links, are the three components to placing your website in the top of search engine results.

When a website receives a large number of natural, permanent links from trusted domains, search engines begin to trust you. After gaining this trust, you continuously build upon it to either gain ranking or maintain it. And if you begin to optimize your website and begin link baiting - you can easily start ranking for competitive keywords, which in turn, bring you search engine visitors.

Continue this method of marketing and your website will undoubtedly increase its traffic. Many bloggers and Webmasters will see an article on Digg or del.icio.us and trust its usability and then reference through a citation link.

Even new websites that start with little traffic or trusted links - will find social link baiting to their advantage and can quickly establish a reputation and begin to build upon it. But just remember, it's the quality of the content that ultimately matters. Content is still king and always will be when it comes to online marketing. Optimizing it in a number of ways will quickly gain you the trust needed by search engines to rank highly, and ultimately deliver the traffic you need to your website.

The Naysayers Are Out There

They're out there. the Naysayers, the ones who adamantly agree that, social media marketing is a waste of time, and brings in useless traffic, leading to visitors quickly leaving after they clicked upon a website. Bounce rates are inevitable - even to your most loyal customers, they aren't always going to be interested. But don't mistakes bounce rates for a lack of interest - if your entire website is relevant to the general interest of a social media website, there will always be a handful of users who will begin to track your website for future content.

Don't forget about the secondary traffic either, which I think is more important in the end. General Websites or blogs with the same interest will link to your content because it helps add value for their users and readers alike. Most of the time, this is done naturally on a daily basis.

Primary traffic might come in larger volumes, but secondary traffic build links from other websites and ultimately delivers their traffic to your website. This help build your brand, establish your presence online, ultimately making it more valuable in the end.

Why you must consider Social Media Marketing?

You could ignore the power of social media marketing, who needs it? After all, you could stick with link exchanges, banner purchasing, editorial ads and search advertising. You certainly could, but why would you?

Social media marketing:

- Is natural. Not only do you get natural links back to your website, it is also is exposed to large groups of people in an unpredictable fashion.

- Successfully mastered social communities can be a great source of web traffic that helps boost your ranking and add to your already established search engine results.

- It's a low-cost/high return business model. If you do it yourself, costs are limited and the only time and expense you have involves hiring freelancers to do it. Ultimately, the benefits exceed the cost - it would take you thousands of dollars to purchase links, which some search engines penalize you for doing now, or are starting to. Social media gives you all of the above FREE!

- Social Media optimization and marketing normally won't interfere with any methods of getting traffic to your website. This new level of marketing will only add to your already established campaigns - and most of the time, exceed them.

So How Does This Make Me Money?

Directly, it won't - that is not how this method works. Your site needs to perpetuate itself and build upon its established exposure. The more supporters you have, the faster word spreads about your website. And social media websites deliver more traffic on a daily basis, compared to all other web communities. Because social media websites can be leverage for links and better search engine rakings, they ultimately increase your website's potential. For example, you will be able to price ads higher or generate revenue from any paid business model.

The Blog Secret

It is as simple as it sounds; an excellent blog will bring you traffic and sales you need to succeed. There is a secret to blog writing and marketing thereafter - it's very simple. Instead of creating numerous blog posts that ultimately go nowhere, just one excellent blog post, which is then pushed through social media channels and emailed to other bloggers through email pitches.

You can write just one post and get an enormous amount of links and traffic to your website through the use of social media.

Social media marketing is not a secret, but to do it correctly and monetize your brand, and bring in the new traffic you need to succeed - it takes know-how and the willingness to 'give in.' Every day, I speak with someone who has interest in social media marketing, but are just not sure of how it might work for them and figure it may not be worth the investment. And that is the exact reason why people don't pursue social media marketing, because they are unaware and are not sure to approach it.

IMPORTANCE OF SOCIAL MEDIA MARKETING

Social Media Marketing - Going Social All the Way

Almost all digital marketing blogs, technology forums and discussion boards were abuzz with news about social media and how it is the next big thing in marketing. It did indeed make a mark, lived up to the hype, and now it is here to stay. Today, it is an integral part of any digital marketing strategy. A few years back, staunch marketing gurus were skeptical about the whole social idea and placed their bets on the tried and tested traditional approaches. Some even considered social media to be another overhyped fad that would generate buzz in the beginning, and die down gradually. But then, there were some that foresaw the immense potential that it could bring. They were optimistic about leveraging it to the greatest advantage.

Cut to present day, almost every business now has a Facebook page, a Twitter account and a presence on other popular social media sites. The word about social media's reach is spreading fast and marketers are leaving no stone unturned to tell clients about the benefits that this medium offers.

Social Media Marketing Strategy & Advantages

The strategy is simple - create an account or page for your business on various social media sites. Talk about your business, explain your product, talk about the benefits, talk about what sets your business/product apart - all using social media. But most importantly, get a professional to manage your account.

As word spreads and people like your product, it is very likely that they will share the information within close circles. For everyone, the circle always includes friends, family members or both. They will in turn share the same within their circles, especially if they like what they see. However, if it doesn't generate the expected results, then you might want to take a re-look at other social media marketing ideas and where you faltered. There could be many reasons why social campaigns fail:

-Sharing too much information

-Risk of litigation

- Choosing the wrong social medium

- Half-baked knowledge

- Hounding and bombarding prospective customers with excessive information about your product

- Amateur planning and execution

The Problem Area

Most people assume that they can market their product on their own since they have some social media account already. Or better still, they think that getting their neighbor's teenage son to do it for them is much more cost-effective idea. Although it sounds easy and simple, there is a lot to it. An in-depth idea about changing social media trends goes a long way in taking the right approach. Sadly, this is where most people fail. "Why do I need to hire a professional when I can do it myself?" is a question most people ask. There are dedicated agencies and professionals who specialize in Social Media marketing Services. They spend a huge amount of time and energy in understanding the trends and identifying the best practices on a regular basis in an ever-changing competitive environment. Get hold of a professional and let them take care of business for you. That would leave you with enough time to focus on what you have to deliver for ROI.

The Advantages - What You Gain

Once you have an effective social marketing plan up and running, you stand to gain:

Easy and widespread access - Helps you reach out to a large consumer base within a short span of time.

Increased communication - You can talk to your prospective customers in a directly using social media.

Brand awareness - More recognition for your brand from every share

Sharing the word - If people like what they see, they share it. The more people like it, more shares you win.

Trust - If a family member or friend shares something about a product, people already trust the information, and are more willing to try out the product.

Earned vs. Paid media - You don't have to pay anybody for people to know about your product, or even buy it.

Inexpensive - Compared to other forms of marketing, this is much more cost-effective and saves you money.

Lastly, if you are relying more on search engines to bring traffic to your website, having an active social media presence helps in better ranking. The more people talk about your business, the more trustworthy and popular it is. In layman's terms, search engines rate this as "very good" and reward you accordingly.

The Social Tools

There are many social media tools that provide specialized platforms like:

-Analytics

-Bookmarking

-Measurement

-Automation

-Blog Marketing

-Network Aggregation

The Benefits of Developing Adept Social Media Marketing (SMM) Strategy

Social media is on a striding upsurge. From swift communication to business promotion, social media is now being used by the small businesses to promote their brands, services and products in the most effective manner. By following a strategic approach, these businesses can reach out to the targeted customer base and enhance their brand visibility in the online periphery. Social media however is no more a platform meant for anonymous virtual interaction, rather it is developing a clear identity for itself. Thus, it is imperative to follow adept social media marketing strategy and create a prospective channel through which products and services can be promoted in the very best way.

Right social media marketing strategy is a good way to connect with targeted customers and at the same time generate better web traffic. There are various social platforms which help the businesses to channel necessary information and the most popular ones are Twitter, Facebook, YouTube, LinkedIn, Instagram etc.

The enterprises evolving with valuable message about their businesses are viable in social media marketing strategy. Providing the right information will enable the online audience to connect and follow these small businesses. The SMM strategy should harp on open discussions and communications via social networks. There should not be any kind of spamming or excessive promotional pitch as this will not help in any way to meet your ultimate business needs.

Investing time to frame distinct social media marketing strategy is the best way to attract potential customers and increase profits. There are many techniques that demand proper strategy formulation. For instance, social bookmarking sites play a decisive role in guiding your SMM plan. These sites help the target audience bookmark, share and vote for your website, thus helping it to reach out to wider market.

Twitter, the micro-blogging website is another effective channel of communication for small businesses to increase their visibility. Twitter gives quality information to your followers and in the process helps establish the brand visibility for your business. Twitter is one of the most vital tools for B2B social media marketing.

In B2B social media marketing, a plan of action regarding how you reach the organization's goal defines your strategy. As you decide to move ahead, you need to harp on certain parameters to form a good strategy. The most essential thing which you need to consider before initiating a SMM campaign is to understand the reason you need to utilize media platforms. Is it for building the brand awareness; is it for increasing sales of for serving both these purposes?

The next important thing is to understand where you stand among your potential audience? If it is 'nowhere' then, your prime incentive must be to make your customers aware about your business. Then gradually focus on communicating with the targeted customer base and potential generating leads.

The next target in B2B social media marketing is to find out the media interest of your target audience and how they tend to use the social media. While some follows RSS feeds or bookmark their favorite sites, some simply uses the social networking sites and the video podcasting sites to follow the stuffs of interest. You must remember that these aspects depend on specific age groups, interests and other social behavior patterns so you need to plan and strategize accordingly to work these interests and turn these into your reward programs.

For creating solid SMM strategy, you ought to know about your company's unique selling proposition. Not the products you manufacture or sell, but find out that one thing that makes your company uni☐ue among the competitors. Define your USP and initiate campaign which speaks volumes about the uniqueness and draws attention of the potential visitors. This is the first and the most important step in creating awareness for your brand.

In social media marketing strategy, it is very essential to nurture your media participation real-time. Social media marketing is all about garnering relationships with the prospective customers in the online realm and this can be done by initiating interaction. You need to provide a human face to your targeted customers to interact with. Blog commenting, forum posting are some of the best ways to carry out effective communication with the online audience.

There is no denying that SMM is necessary for the small businesses for creating successful online presence. However, strategy formulation in social media marketing is not a child's play, rather re☐uires formidable expertise and for best result, it is recommended to hire a professional social marketing agency.

Understanding the Potent Power of Social Media Marketing for Business

Finding new and different ways to market yourself can be difficult. Reaching current and potential customers is easier if you know how to use social media. The following are a few terrific ideas for utilizing social media in your online marketing strategy.

Answer as many questions people throw your way as possible. Take the time to look for these each time you visit your site.

If you need help, don't be shy about asking for it! Although professionals are available to help you with your social media marketing campaign, they can be quite expensive. They can be pricey, however, so be ready to open your wallet if you choose this option.

TIP: Using LinkedIn with your social media marketing strategy is always a smart move. In fact, you can link your pages directly together using a blog app.

Interact with your followers and make a point of commenting on other blog posts. Comment on posts when you have something to offer to help get your name out there. The simplest and most straightforward way to do this is to interact with people who are posting about your industry. This can be a fabulous networking opportunity.

Social Media

TIP: Create a buzz by offering time-sensitive coupons and specials. This will make the customers want to act fast so they don't miss a deal.

Update your social media site often. A lot of social media users expect frequent updates; if you don't come through, you may lose a lot of people. Aim for publishing updates more than a couple times a week.

You want to make subscribing to your blog as simple as possible. Do not put the subscribe button in a spot where people may not notice it. Instead, place it in a visible spot that makes it easy for fans to sign up. Remember that not every online user has high-speed Internet. Therefore, it is best to ensure that the "Subscribe" button loads quickly.

TIP: Give the social networking followers special and exclusive offers. Give your customers something they can drool over, something very hard to find.

There are a few things to consider before you actually market on various social media networks. Each social networking site is different, and knowing these differences can help you to make the best use of your time. You may find you get better results from one site in particular, and choose to devote your time to that one.

YouTube has become a great way to promote your product or service. You can periodically create video blogs about recent updates with your company or new products that you have available. Post the video to your blog and up on YouTube to provide your business with vast exposure to a wide audience.

TIP: Be sure to tell all your customers that you are entering the world of social media marketing. When your customers subscribe to your page, the social network may let their followers know about your page.

In order to get the most out of social media in terms of marketing, add social network widgets to your page. A widget will make it easy for others to follow you. The right widgets will give users the freedom to re-post your content, vote on polls or enter different contests you're holding. It's a win-win for everyone.

If comments are left on social media sites, reply to them. This should be true even for negative comments. When people see that they're thoughts are being heard, they tend to have greater trust in your business. Make sure to respond in a timely manner to avoid making customers feel ignored.

TIP: Using social media blogs to let people know about your friends can be an effective marketing strategy. It might seem strange, but people want to see your connections before they connect with you.

Create new posts regularly. Readers will keep coming back to see fresh content if they know when you will be posting updates. This is also the truth when people subscribe to other publications. Be certain to have fresh, lively content to attract new and returning readers.

When it comes to social media marketing the right way, it's all about the titles. It doesn't matter where you're leaving a post, you should focus on the right type of title. When you have good and interesting content you will see that your visitors will more likely come back and also share your content.

TIP: Look for ways to get your followers to share your information with other potential customers you haven't reached yet. For example, if you're writing a blog post, don't make it so niche specific.

Use the greatest number of media outlets possible to make the most of social media when marketing a service or product. It's well known that Facebook is one of the most popular social sites, but don't sell yourself short by sticking with Facebook only. You will have more marketing success with greater exposure.

The Importance of Online Social Media Marketing

Marketing a business online through social media websites has become a major industry, with more and more companies moving into this business in order to get the most from their company. By putting off the date when they move into these media marketing, companies are doing themselves a serious disservice, and could be leaving the door wide open to their competitors. Getting in early is vital to ensure that you can claim your brand names, and identify that brand with a product, before anyone else does. Leave it too long, and your rivals could have already established themselves through online social media marketing, leaving you having to constantly catch up.

If you have not started to move into online media marketing yet, then you could have a lot of hard work ahead of you. Setting up your company name on a social network site such as Facebook is only the easiest part of developing an advertising campaign and even that can be long, difficult and time-consuming. Some businesses even put out their media work to expert social media marketing companies, who work out the best networks for the brand name and then target these through signing up the company and creating a profile.

Businesses are often worried about participating in these media, because they fear that their reputation could suffer. The answer to this is the majority of big-name brands has been active in online social media marketing for many years and has established their name on those sites. This has only served to increase their reputation and many of their customers enjoy being 'friends' with these companies through these media networks. If you do not start pushing your company forward like the big-brand firms, you could find yourself fighting against a tide.

Many of these large companies work their media sites using assistance from social media marketing companies. These businesses take the pain out of joining many networking sites and their hard work allows the branded firms to join a broad number of these media sites without having to spend too much time and effort logging on and creating their profiles from scratch. In fact, if you want to join the race for social media marketing and advertising, then you should definitely make use of a networking company with plenty of experience in this field, as they can help you to get the most from your online business marketing without having to spend hours signing up to every social networking. Their experience takes the effort out of your social media sites campaign, leaving you more time to run your business effectively.

STRATEGY MUST DRIVE YOUR SOCIAL MEDIA MARKETING

When it comes to your business, you must have a strategy for your social media marketing efforts. If you don't have a strategy in place, you will not to really make good progress.

The purpose of your social media marketing strategy

Your social media strategy serves as a guide that you can follow in order to get from Point A to Point B. It allows you to stay on the correct path for your business and it helps you to increase your traffic with top-quality target audience members. If your business does not have a social media marketing strategy means that you will not be in control of the direction that you follow and exactly where you are going to end up. It may mean that you will be all over the place and you will have the possibility of never reaching your goals (at least, not all of them). As daunting as social media may be to you, it is definitely important enough to leverage because it will make your business become more successful.

Does Social Media contribute to your strategy the way that you expect?

As you are creating and working your social media marketing strategy, it is important that you feel confident about the idea that it is really making a positive change to your business. Your strategy is very important in such a situation and it is essential that you know exactly what you are doing and how you are going to go about accomplishing what you set out to do. If you choose to delegate your business's social media activities to someone else, it is very important that you choose that person very carefully and very wisely.

Actually creating the social media marketing strategy

Your business's social media marketing strategy is very important and not only do you need one in place but you also have to make sure that your strategy is well thought out and effective. Part of what you must include in your social media marketing strategy is a specific approach.

First of all, it is critical that you establish your objective(s) before you do anything else. Without objectives, you will have a very difficult time of getting where you need to be. If you try to think of developing your strategy as something fun and interesting, it will not become a "task" but, rather, will become a pleasurable activity. You will see that it will go smoothly and easily if you use that approach.

Aligning your social media marketing strategy with our objectives is an extremely important second step. You must make sure that you have an established connection between the two. This all ties into getting from Point A to Point B. Without the alignment, you will not make progress. There are many different social media marketing objectives that you can focus your business on. Some of the more productive ones are:

- Generating new leads.
- Dramatically increasing the number of people who opt in to your newsletter or other offerings.
- Promoting a particular event.
- Attracting more traffic to your landing page.
- Promoting your new offerings.
- Paying close attention to analytics so that you can understand clearly how your business is progressing.

Giving credit where credit is due. It is very important to acknowledge your fans and followers who have been nice enough to support your efforts and to pass on the word to other people they know and trust. Express in some way how much you appreciate what they are doing for you and your business. Some of the analytics that you should pay attention to are the number of conversions you have made, how much revenue you have generated through those conversions, and the total amount of money that you have earned through your social media marketing efforts.

Figuring out how to define success, being able to define and measure success is extremely important when it comes to your social media marketing strategy. There are several ways that you can measure that, including:

- Stepping up the number of conversions that you have been able to make.
- Multiplying the number of retweets on Twitter that have occurred.
- Increasing the number of new visitors, time spent on your business's website and the number of times that visitors viewed your page.

The victories that your business experiences should be closely linked to your social media marketing activities, and tracked through the analytics tools. It is critical that you understand that your social media efforts are tied closely to your business's success. If you wish to succeed professionally, you have no choice but to be as active on social media as you can. Remember to be consistent, persistent, and discrete in your social media marketing efforts. It will be worth the effort in the long run. Whatever you do in business, make sure that your efforts bring forth results that work for you.

What Are the Main Features and Benefits of Social Media Marketing?

If you would have told marketing gurus a few years back that social media websites were going to be where all the action was going be focused, they may have looked at you like you were crazy. Today millions of people use social media sites on a daily basis. These types of sites have such an incredibly consistent draw of users that social marketing has turned into one of the hottest and most effective ways to market your business.

Social marketing tools like Facebook are growing!

The main feature of social marketing is to network and build relationships. Plus, while you're at it, you can get your company info out there and establish a solid group of followers the will help spread the word about your company, products and services.

Benefits

With this method of reaching out, you can reap:

1) A network of core supporters. This audience makes this very easy, allowing you to establish a solid group of loyal and dedicated followers for your business. Your core group will then help spread the word about your business, twice the marketing power without costing twice as much.

2) Increased traffic leading to better rankings. While typically it works the other way around, better ranking leads to more traffic. The amount of traffic you will acquire from being on the social media sites will actually cause the search engines to take a closer look at your site and boost your rankings.

3) Environmentally friendly environment. This media makes effective marketing possible without having to spend a lot of money or use a lot of paper. It is all done on the Internet. In this day and age, people look kindly on businesses that make every effort to be as green as possible.

Overall, you might say that social marketing is more effective than banner ads. Banner ads used to be a great way to advertise; however, today they are so common place the most people don't even pay attention to them. This is not true, though, of exciting and interesting content on a social site. That type of content can spread like wild fire and cost you far less.

Great For Marketing Businesses

Everyone likes chatting using instant messaging technology, whether that is on the computer or by utilizing the text messaging functions on their computer. This is a great way to stay in touch with the people you know. Along with that has developed the social media that we have all become accustomed to.

Places like Facebook, Twitter and a large variety of other social media sites have all gained in popularity in recent years as a place where you can connect with other people and get the information out about the products and services others have to offer. While some only use these social media sites to visit with the people they know, using them to market businesses is becoming a favorite way to generate an income.

With more and more individuals finding it much more rewarding to work right from home, this social media medium has great things to offer. No longer are you confined to just one method of making a living, as a matter of fact diversification is taking on a whole new meaning with social media and internet marketing.

Multiple streams of income can be the answer to the age-old question about how to generate enough money to live on when your old **JOB** is no longer there to support you and your family, but how do you use social media to promote your business?

1) Join several social sites, you can find a large list on the web

2) Install the links from your identities on these sites on your blog

3) Begin to make your presence known there by posting at least daily

4) Offer pointers for others who are interested in subjects you know well

5) Become a trusted authority on social media and direct your readers to your website or blog

6) Create videos that can be uploaded on some of the social media sites

Once you have this mastered you will most likely realize that you are creating an income that will last a life time. Learn more about social media marketing and how it can help you start and grow your business.

Social Media Marketing's Growing Popularity - Why use social media marketing?

Many of today's successful businesses have been around for years, long before the internet was a viable option in marketing a product. Although billboards, TV commercials, and radio and print advertisements have been successful in the past, they will not have the impact they once did in today's market. Many people no longer check the newspaper for movie times, they reference online venues. Many people no longer hand-write letters, they electronically draft emails. Many shy away from garage sells when they can utilize Craigslist. While some may resist the facts, this country and the rest of the world relies on technology more and more every day. This is not something to dread or dwell upon; it is something to take advantage of!

For anyone born after 1980, it is easy to notice the growing popularity of social networks and it does not take a genius to identify the direction in which our world's social media market's popularity will continue to move. People from the age of 20years to 29years use social media more than any other age group, with 41% spending 11+ hours a week on social media sites. Age 30 to 39 is the next most fre uent user base of social media, with 37% of them spending 11+ hours a week on social media sites as well. While the younger age groups on these networking sites will be more interested in social status, the older groups will focus on marketing and advertising. Understandably, most people have heard of Facebook, which has become the largest social networking website to date. Facebook has over 500 million users, half of which log-on at least once per day. Among the US internet populace, 72% are members of Facebook, with ages 18-24 seeing the most rapid growth. That is 36% of this country's internet users visit a single website each day. It would be exceptionally hard to find another channel with that kind of impact. Twitter, LinkedIn, and blogs are just a few of the other popular social networks available today, all providing remarkable accessibility to a large group of people.

Social media is the fastest growing marketing tool, and any business not capitalizing on its numerous capabilities could be at a disadvantage to its competitors. Waiting around and not taking advantage of this vastly growing marketing tool is an opportunity that companies are missing. Business is ever evolving and so must marketing campaigns in order to keep pace with the competition. So then why wouldn't someone immediately get involved with social marketing? It cannot be money, as most of these networks are free. It cannot be experience, because anyone can outsource their social marketing for dirt cheap. Most people just do not know. They do not know what it is, nor understand its capabilities. But most importantly, they are unaware of the positive economic growth it will potentially have on their company.

Social media marketing is the attempt to broadcast various forms of media over social networking technologies, plain and simple. A few perks of social media include increased exposure, increased lead generation, gaining of new partnerships, increased traffic, and marketing cost reductions. On average, 88% of marketers using social media have reported increased exposure for their business. Almost half of these individuals who employed marketing tactics through social media for 12 months or less reported new partnerships gained. Users who spent 6 hours or less per week saw their lead generation increase, and 58% of small business owners using social media marketing were more likely to see marketing cost reductions.

The internet is providing this world with new products, capabilities, and tools that have never before been possible. Social media marketing provides the ability to potentially influence hundreds, thousands, or even millions of people for a fraction of the cost of outdated marketing methods. It is the responsibility of today's businessmen to focus on the future of every market and the direction it is heading. Social media is a wise investment for almost any company and will be more beneficial the earlier it becomes integrated within a company's strategic initiative. Social media networking is only going to grow, and my best advice at this point is to establish your brand as soon as possible through these means.

HOW TO BE SUCCESSFUL IN SOCIAL MEDIA MARKETING

Steps to Success in Social Media Marketing

Social Media Marketing is now an essential component of any business's marketing plan. Anyone with a product or service that needs promoting can turn to Social Media Marketing to introduce, share, gain feedback, engage with consumers and ultimately Sell.

Ask any business owner, what or who are your best Quality leads and they'll likely say 'referrals'. Referrals are generated from one person sharing their experience with another person within their **SOCIAL** circle.

And this is the power of Social Media Marketing. By placing yourself or your business in a social space you increase your chance of receiving more business due to someone finding, searching for, reading about or directly being referred to you.

But like any marketing platform there are always certain principles to adhere to and pitfalls to avoid.

WHO?

Any well planned marketing campaign must begin with the question, who are we targeting? If you are an accountant and you market yourself to teenagers how successful will your campaign be? You have to know who is likely to want or even better; **NEED** your product or service.

Once you work out who you're targeting, **EVERYTHING** in your marketing material, whether online or offline must be in total alignment with this target market. This includes the fonts used, images, language style, colors, offers and overall psychology behind your campaign.

If it doesn't, you will likely have little success with your Social Marketing campaign.

HOW?

The next essential step to a successful Social Marketing campaign is to determine how you will reach your target market.

Each of the four main Social Media websites lend themselves to different marketing opportunities. Depending on the type of campaign you plan to initiate will determine which Social website will be most suitable.

The four most popular Social websites are Facebook, YouTube, LinkedIn and Twitter. If you plan to use all four sites to market your product or service, it's essential to have a thorough understanding of each to ensure your campaign will be successful.

OFFER

Without an offer or incentive a Social marketing campaign falls under the category of 'branding'. And how can you measure branding? You can't.

A successful marketing campaign either online or offline should be measurable. If you put 'x' amount of time or money into a campaign it should return a measurable results in dollar terms or leads created.

Your offer must include these elements if it's to result in a sale or lead...

Unique - Why would someone take up your offer if they can get the same or similar offer elsewhere?

Scarce - We value things that are scarce. Why is gold so valuable? It's because there's not much of it.

Expiry Date - having an offer available all year round won't create motivation in your prospect to 'get it now before it's too late'.

Relevant - your fonts, colors, images, layout etc. of your online marketing must be in alignment with your target market.

Qualify - not everyone that comes across your offer will be qualified. In addition to needing the money to pay for your product or service, they must also be motivated to take action today (or whichever timeframe suits your business model).

STRATEGY

A successful Social Marketing campaign must have one or more strategies in place to ensure the target market follows your sales process.

What does your marketing funnel look like for each strategy for each Social Media website? Will you have one strategy that simply triggers interest in the prospect by having them visit your website? Will you have another strategy that goes right for the sale? What about an email marketing strategy that allows the client time to build up trust and motivation to purchase your product or service? Will you have a follow up telemarketing service to increase the conversion rates of leads that come through?

These are all important questions to answer and implement solutions for if you're to maximize the results of your Social Marketing campaign.

Many business owners believe that they simply need to 'be' in Social Media for it to magically happen for them. They believe that prospects will somehow flood through their virtual doors to get hold of their product or service. This simply isn't realistic.

A Social Marketing campaign needs to be integrated with one or more traditional sales and marketing techniques if you're to maximize your results.

Have you heard - social media marketing is all the rage. Many businesses are beginning to finally realize that they need to market where people are hanging out in 2012, and that's at online Internet sites such as Facebook, Twitter, Google+, YouTube, LinkedIn and more. Registering for these sites is free and easy, but, whoa there, don't take the plunge just yet, as you'll need to know the number one secret to marketing your business through social media.

The secret to marketing your business through social media will be the one deciding factor to whether or not your efforts pay off. Reality is that although most social media sites are free of charge, they require a dedicated commitment of time to establish and nurture the proper relationships needed to help properly market your business online. Unless you know the secret, you may find yourself putting in a lot of time and then getting frustrated that you're not getting the traction or results that you had hoped for. Until you know the secret, you may be able to brag that you have a Facebook page, for instance, but are still confused as to how to use Facebook to promote your business.

To properly understand the one thing that will make marketing through social media sites successful, you'll need to clear your mind and try to be receptive to a new business marketing paradigm. The secret will surely test your traditional marketing instincts, and unless you accept that's it's a whole new marketing world out there, your efforts won't pay off unless you're courageous enough to make the shift. Even after learning the secret, you may be tempted to fall back into "old school" marketing techniques. Resist the urge to cling to familiar and comfortable marketing efforts that have dwindling return on investment. Learning the secret to marketing through social media will empower you to brand your business in new and cutting edge ways.

So here it is - the number one secret to successful marketing through social media web sites (drum roll please). "It's the pull, not the push." Let that sink in for a moment. For those who are already marketing savvy, this may strike a chord, and for those who are a bit confused by this simple concept, there's much information to share.

"Push" marketing employs traditional marketing strategies such as couponing, discounting, specials, and give-away. Now this is not to say that these old school marketing techniques have no place in social media, but they should be employed sparingly and carefully. Research clearly shows that when done too frequently, these push marketing efforts are not received well by the online community. For instance, if you're a restaurant and all you do is update your Facebook page with your daily dinner specials, your customers will likely ignore your messages, tune you out, or worse, discontinue the online connection with your business. So there's a chance in that example that the Facebook page may be doing that restaurant more harm than good.

"Pull" marketing is what businesses will find most successful when marketing online. Marketing your business through social media should be done with much respect and consideration for your customers. By providing your customers with lots of valuable information, surveys, games, and innovative ways to communicate with you, you will position your business and brand in a whole different way and establish a much deeper and more committed relationship with your customers. They'll visit more frequently, spend more, and give you more referrals. Your business will become such a valuable resource for them that their loyalty will pay off in many profitable ways. For instance, instead of just posting daily dinner specials, a restaurant could use its Facebook page to have customers share their stories about good times they have enjoyed there, accompanied by pictures of the food. Or maybe have customers vote on menu items each week to feature as a special. Engaging your customers in new ways will help "pull" them in. And that will be time well-spent marketing online.

Social Media Marketing - 10 Powerful Social Media Marketing Tips

1. Use blogging as a means of social media marketing: A blog is the Internet's version of the corner soap box. It is an outlet that can be used by the average individual to disseminate information. The blog is one of the most effective tools to do everything from developing a large following to promoting new products. It is often through a company's blog that both small and large companies get vital information to their customers. If you want to use social media marketing affecting then you need a blog.

2. Use Twitter marketing to promote messages for other users: Twitter has become one of the largest promotional centers in the world which makes Twitter marketing a powerful tool. You will often hear this person tweeted this or this celebrity tweeted that. Twitter is one of the most effective ways to use social media marketing to turn the ordinary into the extraordinary.

3. Use Facebook marketing as a form of online marketing: Facebook has emerged over the last year as the friend everyone wants. Everyone is either using it or trying to become a part of it. One of the best strategies to make use of Facebook marketing is the use of the Facebook fan page and Facebook personal page. The Facebook fan page is one of the must have tools in your social media marketing arsenal. It allows for a direct connection to your fans and customers. It may also be used to develop better overall marketing strategies with the information that is literally handed over to you from your fans.

4. Use YouTube marketing to boost your blog: There is nothing that lights-up the internet like a good viral video. Weather it is the racy Go Daddy videos or other viral videos; they produce a great deal of attention and traffic. A good viral video can make your business enterprise a household name and produce residual traffic for your enterprise for weeks to come.

5. Use Twitter marketing to expose your products to more people: Endorsements have always been a tool of any marketing firm. Big names carry weight and often have explosive marketing power. Twitter marketing and Facebook marketing allow for this power to be tapped.

Twitter can expose your product to millions of people simply because you partnered with a big name personality.

6. Use social media marketing to make money: Blog reviews are another big way to generate traffic, buzz, and sales. It's another form of endorsements and is a great bang for your buck. A good review could yield you 5 times to 10 times what you paid for it.

Be sure that the person producing the review for you has a rather large following so that you can receive the best value for your money.

7. Use Twitter marketing to make giveaways go viral: One of the best ways to make use of social media is to host a giveaway using social media outlets. The simple investment of the giveaway could yield you many new twitter followers, hundreds of new Facebook fans, and build your email subscription list. This is another Twitter marketing strategy that has long term benefits.

8. Use social media marketing to hook up with celebrities

Social bookmarking sites allow you to make a mark that can be stumbled upon later on. Some of the best sites for social media marketing are:

- Digg.com

- StumbleUpon

- Reddit

These sites are great for storing links, organizing them, and directing traffic to your business website.

9. Use social media marketing strategies that are often overlooked: You are probably using Twitter marketing and Facebook marketing already. Instagram and other social networking sites are often overlooked when it comes to social media marketing. The effectiveness of them however has not diminished. It is still a major platform used by music artist to distribute music and other items.

There aren't any major companies that do not have Instagram page, and you should too! There are still people that religiously use their Instagram pages and they make a great target audience for your marketing strategy.

10. Use Twitter marketing, Facebook marketing, and YouTube marketing all together: The best social media marketing strategy is to combine Facebook marketing, Twitter marketing, and YouTube marketing all together. You can have your Facebook fans follow you on twitter while checking out your website.

You can then have the people checking out your website participated in your give away which drives them back to your social media hub. You will have an injection of new traffic from your celebrity connection.

Social Media Marketing Tips For Business

Using social media sites for marketing can dramatically expand the reach of your business. Even those companies that are doing well can derive some benefits from this method of outreach. You will find a variety of tips in this article to benefit your ⬜uest to grow your business enterprise.

Do you want a connection with your customers? Keep your advertising simple when you want to boost sales through social media marketing. If you desire getting on the same level as your customers, just say hello to them! Your customers will let you know where to go from there.

Followers can easily share your content with Facebook. If you receive a comment from someone, it will appear in that person's feed where their friends can see. Encourage followers to communicate online with you, and among them, to enhance your exposure.

Fresh Social Media Marketing Ideas

Special Offers

One excellent method of increasing your followers is offering coupons and exclusive discounts to them. This practice works to improve not only your social media profile, but also your bottom line. Special offers encourage customers to connect with you and to make more purchases.

Use social networks to promote special offers. Facebook users will find more incentive to visit your page if you offer fresh content and special offers. Use social networking to learn more about your target market, including their wants, needs and perceptions of your brand.

You can draw much more attention to your business, nowadays, by taking advantage of new social media marketing ideas. If people start to share comments and review about your business on social media sites, this can be of great benefit to you. Adding contests and special offers to your social media site will give readers incentive to keep returning and spread the word.

Place deadlines on some of the contests and discounts you offer. This can make people in the network more likely to pay close attention and jump on specials quickly, before they disappear. They will likely share these links with their friends and family.

Competition

When looking into building a Facebook page for your company, research how similar companies are using their pages on the social network. When you figure out what you think is helping them succeed, and what isn't, you can adapt your page in a way to succeed more than any other pages you see. Your page should be very unique and appealing.

Create a business account, using your business' name, on both Twitter and Facebook. This guarantees that no one else utilizes your business name when posting or tweeting content that is inappropriate or that has nothing to do with your business. You can use this name whenever you are ready to get into social media marketing.

If an item isn't important, interesting or relevant, it is not a worthy post. Your business should use Facebook to post only the most useful and intriguing ideas. Don't share just anything, just to share. You can share content which is hilariously funny or amazing to watch, but it should always be factual and relevant. Make sure that they are things people will really be interested in knowing. Avoid posting worthless quizzes or anything that could be perceived as spam.

Use LinkedIn and connect it to your blog to increase your marketing prowess. When your blog has the LinkedIn share button, any good content you provide can get spread by your readers, giving you free expansion of your online presence. People will then work for you by letting others know about your blog through sharing. As you may potentially reach 100 million people, this can be a very successful form of marketing.

Commenting

Try commenting on fellow social media blog posts. It is called social media for a reason. That means to be effective, you need to socialize. To increase visibility, simply start to comment on blogs or profiles that are of relevance to your own niche or specialty. It quickly becomes a major networking opportunity for self-advancement.

Content

It is extremely important that your site is updated and posted to frequently. You don't want customers to get bored. Keep them entertained and interested. Determine your own posting schedule, or consider using a service able to post on your behalf at regular intervals. This way, you are always on your readers' radar.

Create humorous content when possible. Keep the humor appropriate, but use it when you can so that you can increase positive reader reaction. Anything that provides humor has a better chance of being shared between friends and family members. This is a really easy way to get exposure.

Share Buttons

Find ways to increase your ability to reach contacts of friends and other users that exist on the social networks. Try putting a "Share to Facebook" button at the end of each of your blog entries. It does take a small amount of time and effort, but the results can be well worth it.

Keep Customers Updated

Let your email list know that they can find you on Facebook. You probably already have a decent mailing list if you've already been marketing for a while. Send a link to your Facebook to everyone on your list. This makes it much easier for your current customers to locate you.

Think about your demographic and market towards these people when you think about social media marketing and maximizing your results. Figure out who is visiting your profile and then make your campaigns even more appealing to that crowd.

Even though holidays usually mean people buy more, you should not take this as a sign that you don't have to focus on your customers. You can inspire holiday spirit and shopping enjoyment by staying in touch with customers during this busy time. Plan the holidays well ahead of time: come up with fun ideas for contests, giveaways or coupons. Your customers will have fun if you promote the holiday spirit.

These social media marketing ideas and tips will assist you in getting started in the new area of using social media tools for marketing. If you make the most of the advice that has been offered here, your customer numbers will surely rise. As long as you devote the time and effort necessary, using social media marketing strategies can be extremely profitable

USING SOCIAL MEDIA TO INCREASE YOUR INCOME

The internet has been a convenient way of making money from your home. There is a wide selection of income opportunities online. Some of which are designing your own website to sell your products or services, another is through affiliate marketing where you simply sell a merchants service or product through links and also, you can sell your products directly online through eBay and Amazon. However, the best way of making money online that most people do not notice although it is already quite popular is through Online Freelancing or selling your skills to employers online. So how does Online Freelancing work?

Online freelancing allows you not only to make money online from your home but also lets you work on your own time. You can schedule a working hours for your freelance job depending on your employers requirements. Unlike your ordinary day job, freelance jobs have no specific skills requirements or any certifications, diplomas, or any manuscripts that proves your specialty. All you need a fast internet connection, basic knowledge on the use of a computer and a few MS applications like MS Word and MS Excel, time, and of course your willingness to make money and learn a few skills online.

Some of the famous jobs on online freelancing are writing, data entry, picture editing, video editing, voice over, script writing, blogging, website management, encoding, rating and writing reviews, bookkeeping, web design, engineering design, drawing, video creation, social media tasks and many more. The jobs present in online freelance jobs are actually limitless and each of these jobs pay higher compared to a normal day job. An example would for someone who writes articles for a magazine in an editorial company compared to someone who writes for an online magazine. The possibility is that the online freelancer is paid three or four times the person working under a company; what's even better is that he works from home and writes at his own pace - no bosses to order him around and no fees from transportation, food, coffee or any sort of expenses.

EARN MONEY WITH A HOME-BASED BUSINESS ON THE INTERNET USING SOCIAL MEDIA & ONLINE SOCIAL NETWORKING

You can earn money on the internet with a home-based business using social media and online social networking with virtually no investment, and advertise your products all over the web for free. There are a lot of legitimate opportunities to start a business on the internet that you can build with more profit potential than ever before.

All start-ups take work, of course, whether it's in the virtual online world, or in the traditional world of retail, restaurants, boutique shops, etc., but one important thing has changed in the past few years. Social networking sites like YouTube, Facebook, Instagram and Twitter have leveled the playing field in favor of the small businessman or woman. In order for many companies to reach a wide audience they have to spend millions of dollars a year on advertising. The average person in business now has access to a worldwide audience that could only have been dreamed about in years past. How can you take advantage of this golden opportunity working from the comfort of your own home and potentially make more money than any weekly paycheck can offer? Here are some tips.

If you are going to start a business from home there are a few things you have to consider. What is the investment; is there training and support, and is the product or service you will be offering something that is in demand? There are several companies, often called hybrid or network marketing companies that offer excellent compensation plans, require little or no investment, and a product line that is both popular and consumable month to month. You can earn money by working from home on the internet if you choose a business wisely, and go about the task of promoting it with the new social media technology that is out there. Do your homework, get started and follow through. You can be successful with a business at home. It's just up to you how successful you want to be.

Using Social Media to Increase Your E-Commerce Income

Having your very own E-commerce site can be quite an enjoyable and profitable activity. Home based businesses are on an increase, but so is the need to effectively advertise. Odds are you currently don't have a lot of money put aside to promote and you are searching for a something cost effective. Social media marketing can meet your needs to improve profits, communicate with your clients while keeping well earned income in your wallet. Make use of the suggestions within the article below to help you to get started out.

The initial step to social media advertising is digging deep and learning the different sorts of social networking sites that the clients at this time use. Typically the most popular ones like Facebook, Instagram and Twitter will always be a good choice, but there might be others available that you might not have even considered! Think about adding a simple opinion poll on your own internet site and questioning your visitors directly about their different choices for social networking sites. This enables you to not only communicate with your visitors but learn a little more concerning this type of marketing.

Competition isn't just there to upset you, but the truth is, they can help you as well! Take note of rival businesses that promote comparable merchandise to your own and look for their profiles on various social networking sites. Chances are you will either discover ways to do something or how not to do it. It will depend on how much response a certain business will get on their own user profile web pages. There are a few businesses that you might come across that are popular from your perspective, but take the time to read through their comments page. Are they still well-liked or are the remarks mainly about unfavorable features of the company? Reading through remarks of consumers will help you shed light on the appropriate and improper things a rival business does. Additionally, it may provide you with a terrific way to enhance your own company's user profile.

Social networking sites are a good way to enhance product sales and offer freebies from your company. Customers you previously had will likely be happy to find out about new items and campaigns you're having; newcomers might discover your products or services by means of this process and turn into loyal customers for your company. Social media websites are really a totally free way of getting your product presentation out to everyone and improve your web page views.

It's very important that as a business owner, you communicate with your visitors and don't simply make use of the web page as advertising only. There's nothing wrong with advertising and marketing being your primary aim, but don't push it down people's throats. Approach this process with careful attention and visualize a good method to market your products which doesn't appear pushy or needy. Individuals don't wish to see somebody that is obviously desperate in attempting to push their goods in the marketplace. It is crucial that you've got self-confidence and respond to comments or publish company news too.

Your social networking web page will help you promote your products or services. A terrific way to accomplish this is as simple as coming up with demonstrations. For instance, lots of scrapbooking artists design page layouts step-by-step then send individuals to their internet sites where these popular items can be bought. This is not merely an excellent advertising strategy but additionally teaches clients something totally new which in turn earns their confidence as well as interest. Provide a new demonstration every week and you're sure to see a rise in product sales in addition to webpage views.

When you have made the decision of including social internet marketing with your E-commerce business, you are making a sensible decision. It is crucial that you continue making wise decisions and stick to the important guidance you've discovered using this article! Doing all of your marketing and advertising right is just half the work; well-planned study can help you go all the way.

Learn How to Earn Money from Home

If you have never worked from home there will be an adjustment. First you have to decide to learn how you are going to earn money from home. There are all types of strategies but they each take a unique approach. It is your destiny. Do you want to learn how to earn money from home?

Four Steps to Set Yourself Up For Success Earning Money from Home

- Establish a schedule. You know what your life is like and when the opportune times are that you can learn how to earn money from home. Everyone that is currently earning money from home started somewhere. Maybe you only have a couple minutes a day that you can allot to your education. That's more than you committed to it yesterday. Do you ride the subway to work? Spend the time learning how to earn money from home. Are you a passenger in a carpool? Become the drive time destiny changer riding shotgun. When you come home from work, do you drop yourself in front of the television for a couple of hours? Couch potatoes may have to miss the latest reality show to find the time to learn.
- Organize your space to earn money from home. Then close the door and get to work. If it's on the subway, have a portfolio. If it's actually at home, then have a door. Depending on the strategy that you decide on will determine how your space should be organized and the file system necessary.
- Develop short and long term goals. What are you trying to accomplish? Earn extra money or make enough money to leave your job so that you can earn money from home full-time. Unique goals direct you towards different strategies. If you have mile markers you are aiming for, then there is something to keep you motivated. If you have decided to devote a limited amount of time to see what you can do with your idea, it is even more important to define what you are trying to achieve in that finite period. You should always be evaluating your strategies with regularity so that you can

determine what is working and duplicate it or figure out what is not working and either modify it or ditch it altogether.

- Institute your own reward system. No matter how large or small your goals are, when you achieve one of the things you are striving for, reward yourself. It can be something small that doesn't cost any money but something you have wanted to do or it can be a trip to your favorite store at the mall. It will motivate you to achieve your next goal, and the next. You have a reward system with your job, it's called a paycheck. Sometimes it takes months to reach a goal you have set to earn money from home. Sometimes it takes less time, other times it takes more. Since the journey will have plenty of obstacles, knowing that you've promised yourself a trip to the spa once you hit a sales figure, puts a pleasurable after effect once you've worked and attained that goal.

The amount of time that you spend learning how to earn money from home will directly affect how much money you actually earn. If you are not willing to learn the ins and outs of a strategy, then it is never going to work. If, however, you make a commitment to learning and then set some concrete attainable goals to strive for, it is only a matter of time before the rewards remind you why you have been working so hard.

www.ingramcontent.com/pod-product-compliance
Lightning Source LLC
Chambersburg PA
CBHW031518210526
45464CB00007B/2966